In this story  short o vowel

words and sound them out?

hot   pop   lot   stopped   not

Here are some fun My Little Pony words:

beach   sand   waterfall

Here are some new sight words:

very   are   of

It was hot.
It was a very hot day.

The ponies were at the beach.
The sand was hot!

"I have an ice pop,"
said Skywishes.
"I like ice pops on hot days!"

The ponies went to the well.
They drank a lot of water.

Skywishes stopped
under a waterfall.
The water was not hot.

"Hot days are a lot of fun!" said Skywishes.